POSSESSING THE PROMISE

JASON W. SMITH
ALBERT B. ALMORE

Published By:
Jasher Press & Co.
www.jasherpress.com
customerservice@jasherpress.com
1.888.220.2068

Copyright© 2015
Interior Text Design by Pamela S. Almore
Cover Design by Pamela S. Almore

ISBN: 978-0692425824

First Edition
Printed and bound in the United States of America

POSSESSING THE PROMISE

JASON W. SMITH
ALBERT B. ALMORE

Latitude Church

TABLE OF CONTENTS

A PROMISE FULFILLED **7**

IT'S OUR TIME **13**

THAT CHURCH **17**

HOME SWEET HOME **23**

RIPENING SEASON **27**

GET YOUR BUTS OUT THE WAY! **31**

WILL THE REAL CALEB **35**

PLEASE STAND UP! **35**

WHY DOES LATITUDE EXIST? **39**

WHAT IS THE MISSION? **41**

LATITUDES TWELVE UNCOMPROMISABLE TRUTHS **43**

A PROMISE FULFILLED

"I have given you every place where the sole of your foot treads, just as I PROMISED Moses. No one will be able to stand against you as long as you live. I will be with you, just as I was with Moses. I will not leave you or forsake you." Joshua 1:3,5

$\mathbf{A}$ promise can be defined as either a noun or a verb. For this series "Possessing the Promise," we will define promise in its verb tense. I believe that my God doesn't just make promises, but that He acts on His promises. The verb tense of promise means: "To assure that someone will definitely do, give, or arrange something; undertake or declare that something will happen." 2 Corinthians 1:20 tells us, "For every one of God's promises is "Yes" and "Amen!" Some of you may be asking, every promise? My response is absolutely!

God has never made a promise and then broke

it. He has never made a promise and not acted upon it. He promises to bless; not curse and to give us a hope and a future. How can we be assured of God's promises and know that we can possess His promises? Let me recap for a moment. On June 14, 2014, Latitude Church had its first "official" meeting. We met in Brent and Nancy Cooper's house for about three hours. This meeting consisted of 17 families and a couple of individuals who said, yes to the call of God to plant Latitude Church.

On that same night, I unfolded the vision, mission and God's vision He had given to me, to be a part of "That Church" in this city. On June 14th, I left that meeting with a promise from God. He didn't promise that we would have a huge church. He didn't promise that I would even have a paycheck. He didn't promise that, "if we build it, then they will come." God promised me this; that He would draw people to Himself, if we lifted Him up. I asked, "What kind of promise is that?" I wanted specifics. I wanted the answers of how many people will come, how many people will be saved, how long will we go without a building, what will our worship look like, who will oversee our children's ministry and what will we call our ministries?

These were all of the promises that I was looking for from God. I wanted real, tangible promises. I knew that God was in the promise keeping business, but with a brand new church and reaching brand new people, I was just trying to keep it real.

It was on the second Sunday, July 6, 2014, that I began to see God's promises being fulfilled. Latitude "planters" met in Cotton Funeral Home and on this first Sunday, the Holy Spirit instructed me to announce that we had to go to two services starting the following week. Two services after two weeks! Who in their right mind would even consider that a brand new church would be going to two services in such a short time?

I thought I was in a dream. God soon showed me that this dream was about to become a reality. Remember, my questions to God was, "how many people and how many etc., will come?" All I could think about was what He had said in His promise; "If I be lifted up, I will draw people unto Me." That is all I could think about; us lifting up Jesus and Him drawing people to himself. That's pretty simple. From the second full service to the next four services, God added over 100 people to our attendance each week. Talk about a promise keeper!

I never once asked God how many again, I just made a point to lift Jesus up. We went from 63 from the first service on June 2, 2014 to 881 in attendance at our "official launch" on August 31, 2014, to an Easter service of almost 1,300 in attendance and now averaging over 800 in attendance each Sunday. All I can say is, "Go Jesus!" The promise that God made to me was this, "You keep lifting me up and I will keep bringing people in." He has shown His promises and has kept His promises. God acts on His promises.

KEEP POSSESSING THE PROMISE

I love the verse Joshua 1:3; "I have given you every place where the sole of your foot treads, just as I PROMISED Moses." If we stop there, we might miss it. Keep reading; Joshua 1:5-6; "No one will be able to stand against you as long as you live. I will be with you, just as I was with Moses. I will not leave you or forsake you." Now that's a promise! I want you to consider this; the next time that God reveals His promise to you, whatever the promise may be, remember you possess it! You take it and claim it. You hold onto it and make it yours. God never gives or makes a promise without knowing that we have a choice to make.

On May 8, 2014, I had to possess my promise. I was sitting on the "Serenity" deck of a Carnival Cruise ship preparing my upcoming Sunday message when it was as if an audible voice came down to me and asked, "Jason, will you trust Me?" I immediately put down my pen, looked out into the Pacific Ocean and responded, "Yes Lord, I will trust you." I followed it up with, wherever, however and whenever I will go. I added one more thing. I said, "You will have to tell my wife!" Answering God is one thing, but telling your wife how you answered God is totally different.

As I sat preparing that message, God began

unfolding His promise to me concerning Latitude Church. I had to make a decision at that moment. I would either possess that promise or miss out on that promise. I had decided at that moment that I wouldn't dare miss out on this promise. If God was for it, who could be against it? If God is in it, then it will prosper. If God has made this promise, He will see it through. If God had not promised it, I would have never pursued it.

There are times in our lives that we stop possessing the promises God has for us. We get complacent and comfortable where we are and we forget about our purpose. All throughout the Bible, we see one common theme; God cares about people who are far from Him. God wants to use us to reach those far from Him. God equips us and uses our stories to be the practical hands and feet of Jesus, while on this Earth.

I don't think God ever intended for us to stop possessing the promises that He gives. He wants us to keep seeking, knocking, asking and doing, till the nets are full! What about you? Have you stopped possessing the promise God has already given you? Are you complacent and too comfortable to keep possessing? I would dare to ask you to prayerfully consider the promise God has already given you and keep possessing it. If you have become okay with just "us four and no more" or the "frozen chosen" please relook at the promise God has acted on and start again possessing. This promise is for your possession.

IT'S OUR TIME

There is a time for everything, and a season for every activity under the heavens... -Ecclesiastes 3:1

Latitude Church-this is our time, our season, our moment and we must seize it now! This is our time to possess the promises of God for our lives, our families and our ministry! As we are quickly approaching our one year anniversary of the conception of Latitude Church, one thing is evident beyond a shadow of a doubt...God is with us! And if God be for us, who can be against us!

Since God is for us, we rejoice with heaven over the 150 souls that have been saved, the 100 converts that have been baptized and the countless lives that have rededicated their lives back to Christ's calling! It's amazing to see where God has brought Latitude Church from our first service on June 29th, 2014 in Cotton Funeral Home with just 63 adults and children in attendance; to where we are now at Grover C. Fields Middle School with two services, seeing an average of 800 people every Sunday! To God be the Glory for the things He has done!

We are excited about all of the marriages that have been healed and reconciled, the 100 (+) volunteers that are serving weekly, not to mention our 25 small groups that are transforming lives daily, our Freedom Kids and Surge Student Ministry; none of that compares to the excitement that we are sensing in the spirit NOW!

God is up to something and Latitude Church is smack dab in the center of His will! We praise God for where He has brought us from, but we praise God even more for where He is taking us to! We will reflect and remember, but we will not relent! The word "relent" means to become less intense or to simply slack off. Yes, God has been good to us, but we have not arrived! Yes, we are growing by leaps and bounds, but we will not lose our intensity for God. In fact we will turn it up a notch! We will praise harder! We will worship louder! We will preach greater! We will serve with more fervor! We will continue to be "THAT CHURCH, until the nets are FULL!!!"

We believe that God is calling, "THIS CHURCH" to go in and possess the land! We believe that God is calling "THIS CHURCH" to go in and possess the promise! Now is not the time to slack off. Now is not the time to stop giving. Now is not the time to hold back, but it is the time to turn it up a notch like never before!

Not only are we getting ready to possess 1732 Racetrack Road but we are getting ready to possess the glory of God like never before! As we begin to possess this glory, God's healing power will begin to possess us! His redemption power will begin to possess us! His signs and wonders will begin to possess us and there will be no question in the minds of anyone watching, that we are God's people and He is our God!

God is already speaking to you through these pages! What is God asking you to possess that you have yet to possess? What is God asking you to do that you have yet to do? What has God asked you to give that you have yet to give? There is something that God has told you to possess that you have yet to possess. There is something that God has asked you to do that you have yet to do. You have put it off long enough. Will you respond to God today, as we position ourselves to possess the promises of God? One thing is clearly evident… "It's our time!!!"

For every one of God's promises is "Yes" in Him. Therefore, the "Amen" is also spoken through Him by us for God's glory. - 2 Corinthians 1:20

THAT CHURCH

Then the LORD said, "I have observed the misery of My people in Egypt, and have heard them crying out because of their oppressors, and I know about their sufferings. -Exodus 3:7

I truly believe that God birthed Pastor Jason for the above scripture as it relates to the church. Everyone is born with a particular purpose in mind. God told Jeremiah that before I formed you in your mother's womb, I knew you. God doesn't just form us just to be doing something, but He forms each of us with a particular purpose in mind. God looks into the future and then He sees a problem and forms a solution, which is "You." Inside each and every one of you is a solution to a problem that God saw on the Earth. When you discover that problem, then you will discover your purpose. Usually, what drives you up the wall are the problems that God has geared for you to solve.

When this passage of scripture was bought to my attention, I immediately begin to think about the state of the Body of Christ. Unfortunately, many sheep are sitting in local churches miserable. They're there just to be there, or because their parents went there, or because everyone use to go there. With all due respect, some of them are there because the Spirit of God use to be there. There are several reasons why people are still there, but the fact of the matter is that they are miserable there as well.

Then there is another group that isn't there. This group was at home miserable, hurt and was dropped. They experienced massive church hurt. They have been taken advantage of by a spiritual leader, overlooked, judged, underutilized, misunderstood, or lied on. The fact of the matter is that they are no longer in church. They were sitting at home miserable, loving God, but hating church. They were praying to God, to let it be "That Church" that would strive to be "His Church!"

God told Moses that the people were in misery by the hand of their oppressors – "Tradition." Tradition is trying to oppress this generation like never before. Many people are sitting in their local churches and are completely miserable because the hand of tradition is birthing oppression in the atmosphere. When asked, why are they still there, many will say, "That it's all they know." Others respond that it's their family church, so they go out of respect. Some simply go because of fear of the unknown of going somewhere different.

Even though God's people were going through what they went through, God told Moses three things that blesses me every time I read it. God says, "I see, I hear and I know." Now, that is somebody's word right there. Just to know that God sees you, God hears you and that God knows what you are going through makes a world of difference in someone's life. You can rest and know that it's just a matter of time until help is on the way!

God's message to Moses was to let him know that help was on the way. God begins telling Moses that He had come down to deliver His people. Moses was like okay and?? God began to talk to Moses because God needed a body to work through, speak through and to lead through. This is similar to a message that Pastor Jason preached. Moses was like, "Who me?" God was like yes, you! God began to use Moses to deliver His people.

I truly believe that God has seen, heard and knows what His sheep have been going through in their local churches. The only reason you are an owner here at Latitude Church is because God has seen, heard and knew the misery that you were going through. Similar to Moses, God chose our Pastor, Jason Smith, to work through and to bring His people out of bondage. Find it not strange that our church name is Latitude, which means "freedom." Every owner of Latitude Church was in a place called, "Egypt" somehow and somewhere. Egypt simply represents a place of bondage. A place where something or someone is constantly trying to hold you back, but on the inside you sensed that there was much more!

Pharaoh would not allow Moses to go worship His God, but by the time that Pharaoh was going to allow him to go worship, Pharaoh told Moses, "I will allow you to go, but just don't go too far."

"All right, go ahead," Pharaoh replied. "I will let you go into the wilderness to offer sacrifices to the LORD your God. But don't go too far away. Now hurry and pray for me." Exodus 8:28 NLT

Unfortunately, that spirit of Pharaoh is alive and well today and is still trying to keep God's people in bondage. Some Pastors will allow you to be who God called you to be, but only if you don't go too far. Some leaders will allow you to praise God kind of loud, but as long as you don't go too far. They will allow you to be on fire for the Lord, as long as you don't go too far. But praise God we are not that church! We are "THAT CHURCH" that God is working through to help bring deliverance and freedom to His children.

Wherever the Spirit of the Lord is, there is liberty! I truly believe one of the many reasons why our Church is multiplying by leaps and bounds is because of the liberty and freedom to "just be." Just be who you are and the way that God created you to be. As soon as people hit our parking lot, something begins to leap on the inside of them and they sense the freedom of liberty. Once they are greeted at the doors with love and smiles, they know that something is different about this place.

They sense that people are actually excited about coming to church and becoming the church. My God, by the time Pastor Corey cranks up the band and begins to sing that first note and Pastor Jason begins to preach; they know that they have found a place of freedom! They know they have found a placed called "home!" They know without a shadow of a doubt that they have found "THAT CHURCH!!"

For the Lord is the Spirit, and wherever the Spirit of the Lord is, there is freedom.   -2 Corinthians 3:17

HOME SWEET HOME

I have come down to rescue them from the power of
the Egyptians and to bring them from that land to a
good and spacious land, a land flowing with milk and
honey… -Exodus 3:8

As God is in the process of using Latitude
Church to rescue His sheep from the power of the
Egyptians, a move must take place. We are grateful for
the locations that God has afforded us to worship, but
there is no place like home! Because truth be told as
grateful as we are for these various locations that we
have been afforded to worship in, many of those
places have served as Egypt with Pharaohs in them.
They have been used to tell us when to worship, how
long to worship, what days to worship and charging us
to worship. But praise be unto God, that God has heard
our cry and that He's getting ready to take us to a good
and spacious land; a land flowing with milk and

honey. Now that's what you call, "Home Sweet Home."

It's this good and spacious land; a land flowing with milk and honey, which started the conversation in our minds about possessing the promise. Because all throughout the scriptures, God has promised His people many things with one prerequisite… that they would have to fight for it! Meaning, that they would experience some opposition, but the promise was theirs as long as they would endure the opposition. Latitude Church, as we continue to endeavor in Project 10K and the establishing of our first campus, there will be some opposition.

There will be some conflicts and some things may not go as planned, but stay in the fight! **We will outlast our opposition!** The same goes for you and the promises that God has promised you. Don't be so quick to give up on your dreams or your marriage, just because of a little opposition. Solomon tells us, "that if you faint in the day of adversity, your strength is small (Proverbs 24:10)." Opposition often serves as confirmation that you're headed in the right direction.

As we will see in the next couple of chapters, even though God promised them the land, the children of Israel didn't handle opposition very well at all. They forgot what God had previously done for them as He delivered them from the hand of Pharaoh. That's why I took the time to reflect in the beginning about the things that God has already done for Latitude Church. We need to use those things as ammunition in the face of adversity. We need to remember that if God did it before, then He will do it again. Same God right now is the same God back then! When you know that God is for you, you're not concerned who is against you.

Learn how to gain strength from your past victories in order to use them in your current battles! This is what David did. Saul tried to talk David out of fighting Goliath, but David gained strength from his past victories to use in this future battle. David began to reflect on how God delivered him from the hand of the lion and the bear when he was watching over his sheep. That occurrence with God back then concurred with David's faith in the now. Latitude Church, let's remember where God has brought us from. This will give us strength for where God is taking us to. So where is God taking us?

I love how God puts it; God told Moses that it would be a good and spacious land. God knows that's exactly what Latitude needs; a good and spacious land. We need a land that is going to be conducive for us to do ministry the way that God is calling us to do ministry. We need a land that's going to be our headquarters as we launch out to reach these 10,000 souls that God has commissioned us to reach. We need a good and spacious land, flowing with milk and honey, flowing with resources for our children in order for them to be able to learn, develop, grow and have a great time in the Lord.

Our children will never grow up saying that they hate church or that church is boring. We are excited about our new and spacious land that was revealed to us on Easter Sunday; 1732 Racetrack Road! Even though we are excited about our new and spacious land, we will not be confounded to the walls of the church. We will not get stuck in being in the building or getting complacent by no means! We have other campuses to launch. We have more souls to reach. We have more hearts to disciple. We praise God for our, "Home Sweet Home," but we won't relent until the nets are FULL...10K baby!!!

Master," Simon replied, "we've worked hard all night long and caught nothing! But at Your word, I'll let down the nets." When they had done so, they caught such a large number of fish that their nets began to break. -Luke 5:5-6

RIPENING SEASON

"Send some men to explore the land of Canaan, which I am giving to the Israelites…" –Numbers 13:2

In the passage above, we see God telling the children of Israel that it was their time to possess the promises of God, but as we later read, somewhere along the journey, their "buts" got in the way. Instead of being possessed with confidence, they were possessed with fear. You will never possess the promises of God, if the fear of Satan possesses you! God is calling Latitude Church to operate in all faith and no fear.

God told them that the land was theirs to possess, but they went out as spies instead of owners! God was trying to talk them into something, but they were trying to talk God out of something. That's why Latitude Owners, we have to make sure we never get to the point where we talk ourselves out of what God is trying to talk us into. Even though this little excursion turned out to be a disaster, Moses pointed out some important things that we need to take with us as we move forward into possessing the promises for Latitude Church.

In Numbers 13:18-20, we see that Moses was concerned about the land and the soil that was in the land. Now this is significant because this portrays to us that Moses understood the promise of seed time and harvest. God told Noah in Genesis 8:22, "that as long as the Earth remains, there will always be a seed time and harvest time." Meaning, as long as, the Earth is in existence, whenever/wherever you plant seeds of time, talents and treasures a harvest will and shall come forth! That is a promise from God Almighty.

It's like Moses was saying even though we're going to a land that's flowing with milk and honey, we can't stop sowing our seeds. Moses was telling the children of Israel that they can't stop giving now because they hadn't arrived just yet! Just because they were getting ready to move into their new building that didn't mean that the principles of giving needed to move out of them!

Just because they were getting ready to move into their 1,300 seat auditorium on Race Track Road, with their large spacious place, didn't mean that they had arrived! Moses needed them to keep planting seeds and to keep giving for the harvest of the other campuses and the 10,000 souls that they needed to reach! This is why Moses asked, "Boy's, how is the soil!"

When you look back over what God has accomplished at Latitude Church in such a short period of time, it's evident that this ministry is good ground! In other words, to plant your time, talent and treasure here in this church is a good investment for your future! When you begin to cheerfully give your time, talent and treasure, scripture tells us:

And God will generously provide all you need. Then you will always have everything you need and plenty left over to share with others. – 2 Corinthians 9:8 NLT

Praise God that Latitude Church is good ground and an opportunity to give in an eternal investment with Project 10K. Praise God for being a part of "THAT CHURCH" that isn't afraid to give! Giving is the least of your burdens and one of the greatest privileges that you will ever have. Praise God for good soil!

Next, Moses asked if there was any wood there. Maybe, you're reading this and you're like what in the world does wood have to do with anything? This is another significant question because Moses understood where there is no wood there could be no sacrifice! Moses was indicating to the children of Israel, even though we're heading to the promise land and to a land that is flowing with milk and honey, don't you think for one second that the sacrifices are over!

Moses was trying to tell his church that just

because we're heading to Race Track Road, in our own facility, doesn't mean that our season for sacrificing is just yet over! Just because we don't have to wake up as early, set-up, break down and move all this equipment back and forth doesn't mean that we have to stop sacrificing! This doesn't mean that we are to kick our feet up and say, "Whew! I'm glad that is over." Because the minute we stop sacrificing and lose our intensity for God, we will go from being "That Church" to being like every other church on the block!

God is not calling Latitude Church to be like every other church! God is calling us to be "THAT CHURCH." "THAT CHURCH" that doesn't mind giving! "THAT CHURCH" that doesn't mind sacrificing! "THAT CHURCH" that doesn't mind serving! "THAT CHURCH" that doesn't mind coming out of the four walls and being visible, touchable and relatable to the community. Sacrifice is what got us here and sacrifice will be what takes us there!!! Boy's, "is there any wood???"

Lastly, Moses instructed them to bring forth fruit because now was the time for the season of ripening grapes. Latitude Church, this is our season to bring forth fruit like never before! What type of fruit, you may be asking? Fruit of lives being changed, fruit of marriages being restored and fruit of generational curses being broken! Now is the time to bring forth fruit of salvation and for addictions to be broken! The soil is good. The wood is there. The season is ripe. The time is NOW, so possess the land!!!

GET YOUR BUTS OUT THE WAY!

We went into the land to which you sent us, and it does flow with milk and honey! Here is its fruit. **But** the people who live there are powerful and the cities are fortified and very large. -Numbers 13:27 NIV

This is where the story gets sad. This is where most people and most churches miss it. They allow their "buts" to get in the way. The word "But" is used to indicate the impossibility of anything other than what is being stated. The word "But" is a CONJUNCTION word that often cancels out everything that was previously stated. You need to understand that "with God" nothing shall be impossible!

If what you see and what you hear isn't in conjunction with God, then it's time for you to get your "buts" out of the way! You can tell from their opening statement, that they were more on a mission from Israel than on a mission from God. As soon as they opened their mouths, you can tell that the report was coming more from man's perspective than God's perspective. The Israelites came back and said, "The promises of God are good. Everything that God said about the land is accurate. Everything that He swore to Abraham that He would give us was true indeed-but." And as soon as they said the word "but", their doubt canceled out their promise.

They were simply saying, despite God's faithful promise to us, the people who dwell in the land are stronger than we are, the cities are fortified and very large and we see "Giants" in the land. Their report was full of unbelief, fear and they had no faith. "We went to the land; we saw the vision, found it good, and God's promises are true, but nevertheless, we can't do it."

If this was a test from God, to test the minds and hearts, as a whole the children of Israel failed the test. Latitude Church, let us learn from the children of Israel and not repeat the same folly that they did. Let us pass our test of possessing the land and get our "buts" out the way!

So how do you get your "buts" out of the way? First, remember, what God said. God specifically told them in Numbers 13:2, that I have given you the land. There was no if's, and's, or but's about it. He told them that it was theirs. From that point on they should have rehearsed and remembered what God said even when they saw what they saw. Never allow what you see to speak louder than what you heard from God!

Even in dark seasons, remember what God has said to you in the light!

Remember, where God has brought you from. The children of Israel forgot all about God's mighty acts that He performed for them while they were in Egypt. They forgot about how God parted the Red Sea for them and allowed over a million people to escape on dry ground. If they would have just took a moment to reflect on that mighty acts of God, they would have been able to detect that this wasn't anything too hard for God to do! When you remember where God has brought you from, you will have no doubt with where God is taking you to! Just like David; allow your lions and bears experiences to strengthen you for your giants! Allow your past victories to give you the strength for your future battles!

Lastly, in order to get your "buts" out of the way, remember, that the battle is not yours, but that it belongs to the Lord. Maybe, Moses should have rehearsed his famous speech that he gave the children of Israel when they turned and saw Pharaoh's army closing in on them. It was at that point that Moses said to the people, "Fear not, stand still and see the salvation of the LORD, which he will show to you today: for the Egyptians who you have seen today, you shall see them again no more forever. The LORD shall fight for you, and you shall hold your peace." -Exodus 14:13-14

Moses and his camp should have remembered those words, "that the battle wasn't theirs, but the Lord's!" The next time, you find yourself in the center of God's will and in the center of conflict; fear not, and just stand still! Understand that God's will is His bill! You have to learn how to trust God with what you know over what you see. If God said the land is ours then the land is ours! If God said that it's our time then it's our time! In the face of opposition and when our enemies come against us, we have to learn how to hold our peace and remember that the battle is not ours…but it's the Lord's!

WILL THE REAL CALEB PLEASE STAND UP!

But because my servant Caleb has a different spirit and follows me wholeheartedly, I will bring him into the land he went to, and his descendants will inherit it.

-Numbers 14:24

As we conclude this book, we pray that it will launch Latitude Church into the promise land. We want to end with this one question, "Will the real Caleb, please stand up?" The children of Israel began to walk in doubt and unbelief. They all brought back a bad report to Moses except for Caleb. Caleb quieted the people before Moses and said, "Let us go up at once, and possess it; for we are well able to overcome it (Numbers 13:30)."

This type of confession of faith moves God. Caleb's confession moved God so much so that God Himself said, "But because my servant Caleb has a different spirit and follows me wholeheartedly, I will bring him into the land he went to, and his descendants will inherit it (Numbers 14:24)." Does your confession move God at all? When you speak, do you set in motion your destiny?

Show me your confession life and I will show you your future. Your words arrive into your future before you do. Is your confession life full of we can't do that, or I have done a building project with another church before and this is impossible to do by August? Are you full negativity? If so, no wonder you dread getting out of the bed every day. It's because you have sowed nothing, but seeds of negativity into your future. These owners and leaders that Moses sent out were full of nothing, but doubt and unbelief. What are you full of? Our question is, "Will the real Caleb's please stand up?"

The Caleb's that have the audacity to see the giants, but still see God and say, "We are well able" are the Caleb's that we are looking for at Latitude Church. Anytime you go into a building project everyone knows that there will be some giants that you will have to overcome; financial giants, permit giants, time-table giants, weather giants and the list goes on. But the key to facing those giants is knowing that you aren't facing them alone. As Caleb was looking in, he remembered who sent them out!

As Latitude continues to look into all that God has for us, we must constantly remind ourselves, who sent this church out in the first place to be established. We know that it was no one other than God Almighty! Jesus Christ promised us, "That upon this rock He will build HIS Church and the gates of hell shall not prevail against it!" God is looking for some Caleb's to rise up in Latitude Church. Pastor Jason is praying for God to raise up some Caleb's in Latitude Church that will rise up in the face of adversity and say, "Let us go up at once and possess it; for we are well able to overcome it!" The time is now! The season is ripe! We are well able to possess 1732 Race Track Road!!!

Until the nets are FULL…10K Baby!!!

WHY DOES LATITUDE EXIST?

Latitude Church exists to reach people that are far from God in an effort to help them become the practical hands and feet of Jesus Christ.

WHAT IS THE MISSION?

Latitude Church lives out the horizontal love Jesus Christ in a real, relevant, and relational way.

We desire to go beyond us, beyond this city, beyond this nation and into the world. We want to reach beyond our capacity, to dream beyond our imagination, and to realize the vastness of our Great God.

Latitude will boast and brag about the lives that are being transformed, not about the numbers we are running. Real people who share stories of what a real God has done in their lives.

Latitude church will never apologize for praising God for all that He has done, is doing, and will continue to do. We will celebrate each and every transformed life through Jesus Christ.

LATITUDES TWELVE UNCOMPROMISABLE TRUTHS

1-All Faith and No Fear
Believing and trusting that nothing is impossible for God, we engage in our faith and do not coward down in fear. We are resting in the presence of God right now.

2-This Calling is Huge
The call of God is irrefutable, undeniable and of the highest of callings. We are serious about God's call because He is serious about us.

3-We Cannot Out give God
We consider it an act of gratitude and an invitation to give generously to God. We give of our talents, our time and our tithe. He gave us His all so we want to reciprocate that gift in all we do.

4-We Are United Under One Vision
We will aggressively defend our unity and the vision God has given us. We are called to multiply the kingdom and not to maintain it. Our owners stand in unity under the authority of God's sovereign Word and direction.

5-It's Not About ME

We will NOT cater to personal preference in our mission to reach this community with the Gospel of Jesus Christ. We are more concerned with the people we are trying to reach than the people we are trying to keep.

6-We Prepare for the Groom

We will continually increase our capacity by structuring for where we want to go, not where we are or have been. We will remain on the edge of our momentum by overreaching to harness strategic momentum initiatives.

7-We Strive For Excellence

We create an experience of worship and a passion for the preaching of the Gospel. We boldly celebrate Jesus that will attract the un-churched.

8-Truth and Grace

We balance our worship and preaching with truth and grace. We are free under the blood of Jesus to extend horizontal grace to our brothers and sisters. We breathe compassion not condemnation.

9-Come As You Are

We are more concerned with the state of your heart and soul than your outer appearance or your economic status. You are welcome here!

10-Praise Confuses the Enemy

We will praise God before, during and after all He has done and continues to do. We will continue to praise Him for His hand of favor.

11-What's really Important

We will capitalize on the essentials and not confuse the non-essentials.

12-The Bride

We will work alongside of God to build His church in great expectation of His return. We prepare for His second coming.

POSSESSING THE PROMISE

JASON W. SMITH
ALBERT B. ALMORE